LETTERS TO AMERICA

Fred D'Aguiar was born in London in 1960 to
Guyanese parents. He grew up in Guyana, returning to
England in his teens. He trained as a psychiatric nurse
before reading English with African and Caribbean
Studies at the University of Kent, Canterbury. He
was Northern Arts Literary Fellow at Newcastle and
Durham Universities, and Judith E. Wilson Fellow at
Cambridge University. *Letters to America* is his eighth
book of poetry. He is also the author of four novels,
the first of which, *The Longest Memory* (Pantheon,
1994), won both the David Higham Prize for Fiction
and the Whitbread First Novel Award. His plays
include *High Life* (1987) and *A Jamaican Airman
Foresees His Death* (1991), which was performed at
the Royal Court Theatre, London. *Mr Reasonable* was
broadcast on BBC Radio 4 in 2015. He is Professor
of English at University of California, Los Angeles.

ALSO BY FRED D'AGUIAR, FROM CARCANET

Translations from Memory
The Rose of Toulouse
Continental Shelf

Letters to America

FRED D'AGUIAR

CARCANET

ACKNOWLEDGEMENTS

Ambit (Bullet; Kamau; Burning Paradise); BBC R4, *Front Row* (Kamau); *Poetry London* (Axe; Sun Rises in Mid-city LA); *Poetry Review* (Claudia Jones; I Dream JB Says To Me); *Poetry* (Letters to America); *Prairie Schooner* (King David Cooks Ital in Port Antonio); *Race Today Anthology* (Body Count); *TLS* (Derek Walcott; Downtown, LA); *Living Stream Anthology* (Call & Response); *The Hedge* #3 (Black Lives Matter); *Terminus* (What I left Out); *Wasafiri* (Calypso). My thanks to Debbie Dalton, Michael Schmidt, Andrew Latimer and Charlotte Rowland.

First published in Great Britain in 2020 by
Carcanet
Alliance House, 30 Cross Street
Manchester M2 7AQ
www.carcanet.co.uk

A CIP catalogue record for this book is
available from the British Library.
ISBN 978 1 80017 008 7

Book design by Andrew Latimer
Printed in Great Britain by SRP Ltd, Exeter, Devon

MIX
Paper from
responsible sources
FSC® C014540

The publisher acknowledges financial
assistance from Arts Council England.

Supported using public funding by
ARTS COUNCIL
ENGLAND

CONTENTS

To Dylan, Aniyah and baba Cruz

ATLANTIC GROUND

Where bones build pace under
Water over grown with currents

Where pickaxes solder sparks
Plunged into such cranial soil

Where sounds collide to become
Muffled blankets by those bones

So that I may scrape them clean
Of their funeral salt holdings

So that all those bones assemble
Pulled together by coral music anchors

To walk once more water bridged so
Dance this blue fabric painted there

By a mind that moves eyes hands
Back forth by and by sea made land

DOWNTOWN L.A.

Dark finds me waiting for a world
Birds bring to my patch of green,
Wings sow light, songs keep time.

My eyes sieve this dark till I make out
Stations in thick night, so many lookouts
Now clarify to settle into their names:

Trees, homes, powerlines, crisscross fences,
All meshed with sky, curved all around me.
Now the first engines unroll linoleum traffic,

My refrigerator shudders at the prospect
Of overtime, two lights over my stove frown
As I count down the years ready for daybreak.

THE BORDER

Everybody took from a circle
What only arms could carry,
Yet this circle never depleted
As you would expect if people
Dipped into a bucket or a vault.

Instead it grew more pronounced
Seemed more circular if such a thing
Exists for a shape already manifest
Readymade for this world, all ready,
A whole world before those people

Gathered, their faces shining with
Conviction, for they know what they
Bring to the circle and what they take
From it, that no matter the exchange
That circle grows by giving them more.

The walk to the corner shop
From the tenement yard
Armed with a shopping list –
Groceries on trust until
Payday wipes the balance
Sheet clean for another week.

Days sharing midday shade
With the watchdog asleep
On dirt, bed of this earth,
Paws sprinting in a dream,
As you watch the day cool
Down for you to join friends

For a game of Catcher or Hop
Scotch – the one where you kick
A dry mango seed along squares
Drawn in the dirt as you hop
On one foot – while you wait
Your turn, watching, this happens.

AXE

Tree scar heal takes
ten years to seal what his axe
opened that three o' clock,
dozen-noisy-crows afternoon,
crow-settled oak, lookout, so
many black fruit out of reach.
Axe-swing, gunfire bark
cracks, splinters spark.

At last her cries stop him.
He throws axe at tree foot,
storms away in a huff.
Tree weeps for seven days
through ant visits, squirrel
laps, enquiries by four
pileated woodpeckers upside
down as if prospecting.

She stores axe in used shed.
What made him grab axe,
aim at that tree and swing
with all his might, several
times, before her pleas
stopped him, takes a decade
to unravel, packed neat,
tidy fold, tree, scar, tell me.

I DREAMED JB SAYS TO ME

I dream JB says to me, Perfect the art of walking backwards
In the open as you explain geography to an oncoming crowd.
We pace on membership treadmills as this unfolds,
Next to each other, we face the same blank wall.
I am too out of breath to reply, so he continues,
There's a word for what we do for free, ignored, anointed,
Persecuted, that word slips my mind. I suspect you know it.
I don't. I shake my full head empty, still breathless.
Can a word stand for anything for any length of time?
I can't hear you out of my left ear, so you need to speak up some.
The clock runs out for both of us, tells us to walk cool.
I want so much from this life yet my life asks nothing much of me.

This body whose hairline shin fracture, shortsightedness,
Manifold hungers keep my mind turning over even in sleep.

1960

Conjecture is everything…
A redheaded boyo dropped
Off by my mother with a nanny
During the week, while my parents
Rotated on the buses as driver
And conductress (as she was called
Back then) with her nutty ticket
Machine whose clickety-clack
Mimeographed mum's heart.

As for dad his ticker stopped
Aged 53, the same as his bus
He aimed down Blackheath
Hill into the sprawling capital.
The year was not as cold as feared.
Carnival was only 2 and the 50s
Passed on its signs, No blacks,
No Irish. They bought a two-up
Two-down, redbrick number.

My year petered out like a wet
Guy Fawkes, left me standing,
Not with a broken heart, but
Stuck up to my ankles in data
From an era where a stranger
Looks into my pram and tells
My mother that my red hair
And brown skin made me a
Bloody freak of nature.

WHAT I LEFT OUT

I said watch this shoemaker, his wife, called, Teacher, and a
punishment cupboard
papered with wire brushes that can scrub flesh off child bones. I
added how us sprigs learned by rote, sometimes in a spellbound
singsong,

class follow-along or else ting-a-ling. Teacher's sergeant major
call of someone's name, fresh cut whip flexed in her ample hands,
drew our breathy reply, all eyes on that pliers of a bendy weapon
whose invite nobody cared for.

I left out the fact that I found what
jumped out her mouth to be good
without knowing why, that when
she said, times tables please class,
the whole of us began as one throat
with a few stragglers who skipped
to catch up but kept on with mouth
mimicking to avoid detection by her.

I left out the smell of old leather
whose milk warmth lulled us.
And the old man moving in shadow
seen out eye-corner, head facing
front, his worn hammer that spoke
by measuring, sometimes, the way
we said something, as if to help us
along the path cleared by Teacher.

Enough about that oblong cupboard
she threatened to lock us in for a time
if we failed to tidy letters, square numbers
or got in the way of her forced teaching,
The cupboard of a thousand brushes,
all of them recounted in my sleep,
if count is what I redo when I rock
from side to side at their sight.

A child locked in with those brushes made the sound of a
soul lost for good,
nothing like the balloon, yellow, my first, that I spent my
lungs blowing up only to let it slip
from my grasp and zip around the room until empty.

Not to mention the bouquet of skunks, seven cubs plus
mother, bathed
by streetlight, making tracks down the narrow neck of an
alley, as though beings on that scale
could be arranged in a vase by an unseen hand.

SUN RISES IN MID-CITY, L.A.

Call for wings, alligator skin, eagle eyes, dog ears, leopard speed GPS coordinates if body ever hopes to slip that helicopter whose searchlight combs late night revelers, two-job commuters, down in Arlington Heights.

Ripe for sprawl, mechanized dust, engine backfire or gun, cause drum an' bass sweet so, wild so, madness take over and you muss tek a draw, buss an' lick shot to rass, hence the sky patrol, cloud from countless pistons,

lands inside screens, coats laptop keys, prints fingers, spackles this chance to sit alone before things rev, crescendo, old me, oh my, surrounded by twisted palms flat against three of four skies, their honkytonk blue,

poised for squawking parakeet pinball machine flyover, as all things stop, twist, turn, look up, follow their zigzag, cut, bob and weave, scattergun plantings among palms, if body ever hopes for more than –

potluck green flurry, brass instrumental warm ups, their blessing of a life lived noisily serving animal flimflam, flux, speed, in good, quarrelsome company.

Call for wings on these mornings, temporary ones to join a crew bound for the next best feed amid high-topped perilous, aged-outside-the-cask trees, just to shoot, oh, well, yes, the breeze, among sheltering royals,

at sea, their held-breath, firework branches burst, splay, under jet belly, crisscrossed skies, ink, pong, made by this splurge, cough, spit, concrete graveyard don't give a flying fuck city! Yo! Unheeded camp cry to commerce

whose plugged drains, traffic-light eyes, shuttered noses, stuffed mouths
signal indifference to people huddled in doorways, beside shopping carts
laden with their last precious bundles tied with frayed twine.

Music crowded at my birdfeed helped by a tinny fountain, versus wind-up
wake yu-all jive, hustle for a dollar dustbowl conurbation. If body could
ever hope, only not-I, but me, you, us, them dread could isolate, pl-ease,

selected engagement with this city, sky that just happened, might be
a happening thing, pierced by palms on a growth spurt to some more
opulent heavenly place,

where shopping carts fill for all and one door opens to another in a haven
free of locks, guns, sirens, scalding dust, where splintered I, bifurcated lens,
wait for that flock, come now, up close, here, not just for me.

Skip stone, tiptoe-bounce across lake, no sound as lace tears, struck
match flare view lasts till water mends, no scar, no trace of that flat
stone our child dream slings, awakes to cut-grass smell, salt taste,
bell sound, sponge feel, meteorite afterglow, bruised enamel basin
balanced on head, spills cannonade underfoot.

First time she cries in full, for nothing, this slips out, at last, she
faces up to cancer, owns it, deadpan, she says, her eyes soak cause the
blasted transistor just broadcast Mahalia Jackson dead.

Mother tries to tell her eldest about his country upbringing. He cuts
her short. Not loud, nor long. He puts little weights on each word
fired right at her for all to hear who care to see with hands over eyes
and ears all these years.

You weren't there.

Her local cooking laid out Sunday for seven children, what a spread,
rice, plantains, beef stew, fried potatoes, left untouched, that day,
uneaten, as everyone dearly departed.

Here comes her favorite Al Green LP to spur us in our chores. Let's
Stay Together. She sings and sashays with Hoover. Sometimes one
of us, as we pass her, twirls with her in passing. Let's not. There is
marrow in those scraps on that tin plate.

Leaves boiled for a condiment soak woven bandage. Dogs, cats in
alley maybe play despite howls. I should not ask anything of you.

The sky invites me in for a plunge. Cloud may well suffice for skin, clothes, UV protection. This morning parakeets swirl, their hullabaloo, the fruit of their mass landings in palms feeds, fills, helps closes my eyes for fitful sleep that comes little and light these days.

Try what light does for size.

Burns. Moves on. Leaves no trail for others to follow in its silent wake. Why model myself on a suicide? One feather dropped by a flock on its way to some other republic where everyone dances.

A man asks for change to buy food. I give him the rest of a meal in Styrofoam complete with plastic forks that carry more flavor than my leftovers.

Stop your start eating fast food. Tricked by frying bacon. Vinyl made an improbable return, in psychedelic colour. VHS next? No. Yesterday, my troubles seemed, well, frighteningly near.

Grandfather planted a coconut grove for Grandmother. His shovel spiraled from her grave where he reserved a plot beside her for yours truly.

At any point from about one hundred yards, catch a glimpse of white, head towards it, come upon two cement oblongs side by side in the middle of a coconut grove, what the 60s call groovy.

Come rain, dry nuts slap down burrow mud, plant themselves, wait for us to collect, grate, add sugar, bake, or shell, lay out by road in sun. Squeeze for oil.

We call the young ones, 'growee'. We tear their green hearts from them with our bare hands. Taste of honey makes us look hard at them to find where so much sweetness comes from in so small a thing, in so ordinary a place.

We know to take one or two, no more, know that the grove relies on us settling for a taste, no more. We drink green ones ignore the dribble on chin and neck and chest, just to keep that head-thrown-back slake.

Who cuts spoons from green husk?

We scrape translucent flesh from shell. Uncle so-and-so who rules us with a look leaves us as we keep watch to see a star fall, make a wish to fly abroad, that same hard look finds me here on my toes reaching for a top shelf where I left a stone filched from lakeshore, stashed there for safe keep, until now.

BLACK LIVES MATTER

brings us to this day on a dead-end street, face-to-face
with a young rabbit, no bigger than a tangerine,

blue jays pick up with articulate claws, fly four floors and drop,
but lucky nine lives rabbit lands, thud, looks hurt,

stays still for seconds, as if lost in dream space,
staggers away, and another jay grabs it, until we intervene,

shoo those blue jays into treetops, and wrap
the pulse of fur, with two dimes for ears, in an old T-shirt.

Too young for us to feed it carrots or lettuce, we know
that we must release the bright bulb of a creature back

where we found it, but not before we chase
those lingering jays, place shirt gingerly on dirt, watch that

fur ball flick away into tall, abandoned, lot grass,
as if that bulb lost its element and left an afterglow.

We wait as jays circle, then tip wings for another zone.
We retrieve that tee, its smell of game, and tiptoe home.

BULLET

The classroom, heard. A smell of bodies roomed in. Some washed, perfumed, others fresh from beds that they shared or fell into late, rushed from to get to this class on time. One voice at the front of the class but not in one place, roaming. Others in hushed tones.

Feel it. The thickness of being in the know about what is about to happen in that place. Sunlight sharp with this knowledge. I mean the feel of things as the last thing you will feel. That room, corridor, stairwell, and my approach. My cut, through matter, to meet material, moving or stationary, inert or alive, until I grab them, change them, by our meeting. Split wood. Crushed bone. My work.

Most people get out of my way, but not him. He throws himself in front of me. I oblige. I must meet him in my given role. Flesh of his flesh that parts for me. In a room made for learning: desks in rows, chairs scraped on wood floors, flesh slouched in place.

Come for me, might be what each says to me invitingly. Or so I take the space with them in it to mean by their arrangement. Learn from me. Light split as many ways as sight. Heat of mine to warm insight as learning comes to an end by my hand.

Her as well. Before I feel a thing. She sits in a chair that she fills to capacity with muscle and bone crafted for a basketball center. She breathes life into her desk and chair by taking over them, taking them under her embrace, her breathing. I look in a room full of people and she jumps out at me with her living furniture embrace. I have to find her as fast as I can get to her.

Those two singled out of a crowd. Old man. Young woman. But each one speaks to me in ways I intend to delve into very soon. I wrestle from each of them what each covets. I owe them an explanation. I do not go to them, I am sent to them. Once I launch, I have to fulfill my coordinates, no matter what I think along the way.

This youth carries me from one place to the next and directs me in my work. His hands steer me from one building to the next and along corridors from room to room. At some point his single mind folds around me so that I become a part of him, and no one can tell us apart. He hardly says a word to anyone but me. His thoughts, if counted, add up to nothing but me. I am that boy.

Outside this one room with the two of them inside, the teacher, the student, and many others. They know I am outside and they try to bar my entry. The teacher, retired and teaching his favorite class, mechanical engineering, his pet theory slotted in with a history of discovery about movement of large bodies through air, how resistance and the heat generated by pushing through air at high speed, such limited mechanics, how it left civilization in a quandary with nowhere else to go, unless science invents some quantum new way of generating speed which can be reconciled with delicate flesh and blood, and so he drones on, not a drone, since his voice is akin to music for those in the room, but sonic of some sort which instills quiet in the mind. I speak for him now that he cannot account for himself.

The student, among peers, behind her desk, slouches in her chair. That is how I see her just before I begin to break into that room that the teacher bars with a desk that he braces against with the help of two students. Others leap out of the second floor windows. Limbs break. Lungs fold under concertinaed ribs and air takes a while to find those spaces inside bodies.

I fly through wood doors, walls, curtain or blind covered windows. He is an old man. He knows aerodynamics. He knows a lot about me. We are introduced. But it is a meeting he will never remember.

Why should he? Who would want to remember such a thing? There is no skull able to withstand such pressure. Just as the walls in those classrooms corked ears against the noise of my work. Floors with a lay me down and lay anything on me outlook, tried to turn away from me. Ceilings that boast of vaulted memories found my offerings too much to contain and almost burst their rafters. You see these things are viewed as dead already, as somehow beyond the world of flesh and blood and I note their response to me to convey how effective my work is among the living.

Take the old man, for instance. He has nowhere to go but to greet me as I seek him. Not an ounce in him can hope to withstand my arrival and yet he turns towards me rather than run as he instructs his students to do moments before I reach the door of his classroom. He seems to know what I stand for and therefore he decides at that moment what his life must amount to, if anything. I salute him. We embrace. I cut him down.

As a lover would her competition, as a mother would the first threat to her child, as light cuts down dark, as the sun slices through earth, so I come to you, old man, young woman. Step aside, let me do my work, or be the first to fall.

BODY COUNT

Turn right out New Cross station
    left onto exhaust fumigated A2
        outpace inching traffic
            dodge a cycling youth
                barreling along the pavement
                  look up at plaque
              down at how far each jumped
            chased by deliberate fire

        bass drives blood
    drum fuels pulse
lightning through brain
    blood writes history
        timed on pulse
            shock waves brain

            if one police in each station says
                'no more chokeholds on my watch
            no more hearts stopped on my beat'
            how many Black lives will that save?

    Do the math
    add one to one hundred
take away ten black people
    divide that by two enquiries
        what do you have?

        Our children cry murder
            mothers and fathers lower them
                between two shifts balanced
        on shuffled bills

                        earth receives them
                as earth must without grudges
            balance sheets
they fall
            through our arms
                    held in entreaty
                        we lose their names
                            they become offerings
                                altars made on their behalf
                            spray painted and smashed
                        we lose them we lose ourselves
                    along routes with too few signs
            marking where so-and-so fell
on such-and-such a day
            for no more reason than black
                    skin to his or her or their name

                    we turn on ourselves too
                        from the wrong post code
                            on divided council estates
                        this crew against that
                    we start each day nursing
            insults and reprisals
            blown up as big as history

we forget to answer to our names
            since we do not recognize ourselves
                    you/me/I/we/they/us/them/their
                        peel from our bodies
                            left naked in public
                                for eyes to cover
                            nudity that stops traffic
                    skin clothed with eyes
            pores smothered by hands

history feeds on our bodies
history rolls our eyes
   dips our shoulders
      curves our backs
         we run on bones
            laid by history across oceans
               ask that child on that bike
            if history counts for much
         in a life lived at this pace
      standstill traffic
   web turnstiles
knife wars

   that child cuts eyes at you
      as if you spoke in tongues
         for the sacred whose bones
            pave Atlantic roads
               for those beaten
            choked
      by fire
      by police
   breathe now
underground
   underwater
      over us all

      for the island borders
         our dreams of Africa
      the Caribbean
   South Asia
Europe flows
through our veins
   we breathe spoors
      from Africa's Harmattan

our tongues splinter
    to keep up with dialects
        stored in the roof of mouths
    in the small of our backs
  instep and crook of elbows

  cycling youth
next time you pass the house
on New Cross Road
  stand on those pedals
    balance two wheels on the spot
      spit streetwise praise for those
      thirteen dead

        they move beside you as hard
      as your shadow your footfall
    as soft as your tongue

  bow your head to them
 look back Sankofa-style
along oceans
  whose roads
    call you
      by your name

CLAUDIA JONES
for Carole Boyce-Davies

Trinidad's buss-up-shut*, kiskedees, casuarinas,
Girl, come carnival, what a fete, the whole island
Swinging, streets jumping to the pan, kept you sane,
Awake almost one year jailed in New York, why?

Talk runs something like this: an owl calls out,
You cannot see it but you know it has to be out
There, somewhere, if only you had night vision.
You learn to mimic that coo-coo-do-do so well

That owl answers you as if you might be its mate.
Well done, Claudia, you belong to the clan of owls,
You know what it takes to make owls coo-coo-do
Just for you as you did for them so they do for you.

Thing is someone high up on another perch higher
Than all those owls takes exception to your call,
Their response, and with all the might on the right
Side at someone's beck and call, they seize you,

Claudia, banish you, to another high and mighty
Location for you to launch once more, your vocation
Of calling to owls and all the owls within earshot
Answering your call, just as before, coo-coo-do-do.

Which brings me to your resting place, left of Karl
Marx as Carole highlights in her book to mark you
As one of the lost ones whose call matched any
Number of owls but whose race and gender did not.

Claudia, call us as you did before. Remind us what
We need to hear at this time more than ever.
We are perched in the trees, ears inclined for any
Current sent by you our way, no longer afraid.

Paratha roti

MARX IN THE JUNGLE

Stands under a big top –
Branches clasp hands tight
As tarp, mute light green.

Marx exhales what bad
He can, that leaves inhale,
Convert, turn out good:

Drizzle manufactured
By trees gets under skin,
Puts even teeth on edge.

You step from shadow,
Rain, dark green,
Out into brazen sun

Divided by a line
You dare step over
As much as through,

From wet to dry
Cool to moist light,
Jungle swirl to city grid.

So it is I bring
Your divisions,
Marx, to this sum

Where a border
Might be the waterfall
Warrau children

Dive and invite you,
From their perch,
To join their giddy

Leap into whitewater
Surface, splash, climb
Back for another dive,

Border you crisscross
From one of three
Guyanas into Brazil.

How to tell two nations
Apart, while between both?
Indivisible light, water,

Air, land, conspire, help
Marx roots spread far,
Wide to bolster trees.

KAMAU
(i.m.)

I hear you
As I follow your page
As a child you woke to light
Splashed on walls/ceiling
That drew you to lean out
Your window to face a beveled,
Mirror sea held up to the planed line

Of the horizon
That line curls as your voice
Joins a queue of waves
Taking turns to stand tall,
Charge the beach, crash,
Tumble pebbles

Your voice for a sea
I wade into
Drawn out deeper
By its tug and pull
Until the tide of your voice
Soaks every pore
Makes a xylophone of my ribs
Spine
Nails
Teeth

Taking me back to our drive in your jeep
Up a rutted trail in Jamaica's blue hills
To your small coffee holding
Back to your papered New York University flat
And your return a stone's throw from that blue-green

Lightning glass ruled by eyes
Ears
Nose
Tongue of the sea

History poet
You sing your way through time
From Africa to this Caribbean
Basin where some body treads the sea
And hands beat a ribbed scrubbing board
So your Barbados shines
Back at Africa

Your way of skipping stones
On wrinkled water for a walk
Across the sea
To sink thought
Spirals sent deep
Where all hearts meet
Slip time

Where tongue
Lips
Breath
Skip now

AGRARIAN DREAMS

Map poured from light
Strained, left to settle.
One plain, one upland,
Hills you cannot touch
Or claim, (too steep,
Rugged, slated) except
Stare regularly at them,
A lowland and backland,
These last two in a tier.

Our heroes set out,
Arm-in-arm for a day's
Work in those uplands,
Just beyond backlands,
Not as far as several
Replenishing, standoffish
Hills, uplands, named
For abrupt rises, uppity,
If you will, that demand
Root crops cling, hold on

For dear life, hills sluiced
To coax rain sideways
Downhill. Some crops
Hang on vines, set up on
Trellises arranged in rows.
Others flourish in turned
Ground so shallow a tug
Uproots them. Others still,
Flower as if meant for eyes,
Nose, would only grace

A dinner table if arranged
In a California Faience vase.
Ask Colby Brown, he knows.

How long will they last?
Not those flowering crops,
Or those vine fruit,
Or the ones underground,
Hiding from their purpose.
I mean our happy couple,
Made happier by their love,
Kept happiest of all people
By their line of work –
Outdoors, among scenery,
Close to hills, running water
(Left out of here, so far)
River that's close by,
Lower, if down applies
To land below downlands.

Current twists its rope.
Lovers bathe, for things
Look slow (in fact, farms,
Though always busy,
Induce a slow mind state
That springs from
Watching crops grow)
An impulse that surfaces,
Perhaps to justify –
If reason shapes need –
This afternoon swim.

You might expect much
Farm machinery to support
So many varieties of crop,
And so few hands around.
Look for more than a tractor
With attachments lying about
And your search will be,
How shall I put it my friend?
Fruitless as a mud pie,
Amiable as a cowpat.
For one tractor is all there
Is and it sits idle growing
Rust, cobwebs, this certain
Air of disdain for such
Willful neglect.

Are people hired from miles?
Who trek to the farm
Only to disappear at dusk?
Is there a shadow population,
Hard to spot, but secreted
Among roots, vines, cornrows?
Maybe they keep low for lovers,
At work and play all over
Those lands, I mean, up, down,
Even in the middle, happy
Lovers, described as such
By most, for whom desire
Breaks out, a hunger for each
Other anytime, anywhere,
That requires the discretion
Of others, hence those secreted
Workers who keep low,
I cannot say for sure. I only see

Farmlands and two lovers,
Visibly happy at work and play,
As if the two activities
Were one and the same
Way to keep bodies pressed
In service to love.

Add light to land, as light
Falls and rises, both,
Through the open hands
Hills hold out, into the lap
Valleys spread, onto the face,
Now crinkled, now smooth,
A river turns skywards,
That reflects light back,
Right back up to those hills,
Light that seems to operate
All the moving parts
Behind those lovers smiles.

KING DAVID COOKS ITAL IN PORT ANTONIO

I

Sun softens asphalt to lava islands around potholed stone roads.
We climb zigzags cut willy-nilly into hillsides, by rain, goats,
Tree roots and barefoot hill dwellers. King David tells me a toad

For a man, slapped him with a cutlass, and for days croaked,
Outside his house, Rasta come out and face me. But King David
Says to answer that call and wet his cutlass with another man's blood,

Not his way, so he left that town for this other dungle. He divides
His attention between his mobile and me. He hails his neighborhood,
Left and right, Ayah, Dread, blessings, me see you, peace to all.

He whistles at shacks to let them know he trespasses, lean-tos
That cling to rock shelves, waves of zinc roofs, hardboard walls
With square cutouts, propped open by staves, serve for windows,

The whole contraption planted on a concrete base, if lucky,
Or on four concrete blocks. He plucks passing leaves that his fingers
Worry into a paste, ranging from conditioner for his covered locks,

To backache remedies, to blood cleansers, to a cure for chiggers.
He shows me his place, no electricity, no running water. No more
Than a single car crate, and a square lookout for green air.

I take in his worldly goods in a glance and back out the door.
He figures modest dollar amounts he needs to run a pipe and wire.
I stand by the entrance and wait for him to collect what things

He needs to give to a friend to take to a relative off the island.

A banana tree angles upright in the steep yard, another thin
Guava tree, laden with tightfisted green fruit like garlands,

Destined to soften and smell up the place and bring plenty bird
Noise and nosy children, and through lush vegetation, a glimpse
Of the sea, planed to perfection. All around stand a herd

Of similar shacks, variously sized, all uniformly poverty rinsed,
The colors run into each other; most mixed and matched.
I wipe sweat from the climb but more spouts for what I fear

More than cancer or robbery at gunpoint: I come from their batch,
People with nothing to their name, just like how I was reared:
A love with nothing to its name coursing the veins, a listening pulse.

The hill overlooks the sea of Port Antonio. Water with sky
Soaked in it, glistens as if to fulfill any and every impulse,
Numberless coves shine with jewels planted there to satisfy

All our cravings. But the precious light, brittle really, plays
Tricks on me, and shifts from one shape to another as I cling
To my wish to transform these choked hovels on display,

Into safer houses, sturdy retreats, and homes fit for kings.
It is a crude wish for King David that I make as he ducks
Into the open, cups in hands with wine he brewed from fruits

He says he picked here (he sweeps our surroundings with a tuck
And lift of his chin) and set months ago. I sip the spirits
That sat for so long small bubbles percolate from black tea.

I nod as my tongue and nose register perfume and paraffin hits.
He wants to cook ital for me in my rented kitchen by the sea
Where injured French sailors rowed ashore to evade the Brits.

2

We clamber down the hill and he warns me, in our stop and go
Progress, to mind a spot erased by rain, or blocked with undergrowth,
I ask him about his limp. He sliced his bare foot picking a mango,

Said he unwittingly stepped on a half-buried piece of rusty hoe.
He cleaned the gash and stemmed the blood with coco leaves
And green banana peel, heated, and applied in a poultice.

I moaned about my sore heel earned as I hopped waves
And dropped hard on a flat stone in a sun-hurdling race
With my two sons, from prone on sand, one moment,

To a driven buoyancy, salted and cool, the next. He regrets
The lack of capital in the place, more tourists would foment
Commerce in a parish that's Jamaica's biggest secret!

He wields a knife with blind expertise and slices balanjay,
Callaloo, onions, cabbage, tofu, and keeps three pots
Simmering and me running on fumes in the kitchen as I DJ

All my classic reggae on my Mac. He chops and sings, nonstop,
Raises pot covers like cymbals, stirs, and puts them down
Quiet as if changing his mind about clashing them to the beat.

He offers my family this land on a plate, its jewels, with a sound
For every mouthful and me wishing more mouths on us to feed.
We give thanks. He holds a pineapple upside down and peels

The entire thing and carves out the pocks without touching it,
Leaving flesh decorated with tracks he could add in his sleep.
Seated and full, he talks about the dreads that are hypocrites,

Who say, burn money, smoke white people, fire cocaine, but
Indulge all three when they think no one looks. Me love everyman,
He says, but if somebody nah love me, let him stay put

Over there and I man stay here, no problem. I give him what I can
Afford and he steps out into pitch and heads for his sliver of hill,
With a song and cut foot dance he surrenders to night, thick as trees,

Stuffed with insects adding to the score of tides. I hear him still,
Belly full, yet he keeps a hunger my charity cannot appease.
To clean up Little Colombia (Port Antonio's street moniker)

Whose shipwrecks under dark cover, weighs and parcels out cargo
For high streets, that fills jails and graveyards, police monitor
But cannot stem that tide and politician campaigns embargo.

3

If King David grasped the advising rain here, he would have left,
Flown off one of many promontories where the surf breaks
With history: voices lost at sea coming ashore over and over, bereft

Of a resting place, they crawl up the beach with nothing at stake,
They do not even leave crab tracks, some lodge between
Stones where an ankle caught or the fear of leaving water for land,

Where bones turn ground only to become powder and flesh streams
Off bone through skin sack stretched more porous over time bands.
His patch of cove light and water mining diamonds and pearls.

His wingspan of fenced soil for him to sow and reap all things ital.
If man can make it in Jamaica him can make it anywhere in the world.
He says, do not under, but over stand, hell is low, so says hi or hail.

He stays because he believes in the light that falls free of history.
The fool fell for sunlight's stones harvested at sea, a pirate's bounty.
A pot of gold at the end of a strained rainbow, a mermaid mystery.

And no proof for any of it if you comb Jamaica's three counties.
Hills push up against each other in courtship and pull up long skirts
From the swing of the surf, but lean over to look and see what happens

Just over the floor-length hem of a cliff where birds ride unhurt
By the current of history. His natural curiosity keeps him lapping
At the milk offered by full moons, loving mountain air as much

As sea breeze, wanting both in one life and so stuck with compromise.
He cut off his locks once when a friend tricked him into eating meat.
He cried out of puzzlement about his next step in a life that promises

Nothing, with no time for tears, so when his eyes dried he greeted
His new conviction to regrow his hair and never uncover his head,
Follow any man, or movement, except the wise counsel of his soul.

He heard a voice inside him say that he should be his own dread.
He left that town as well and thinks Port Antonio was always his goal.
And that is the first step of madness, to believe you can defy the law

Of gravity and walk off a cliff, or understand surf speak, or brace
Against a mountain whose bulk harbors its separation from, and draw
Towards, sky and sea, or if he smokes he gains wisdom and grace.

Or that he can answer the growl of his belly with drum song. No, say
The silent planes of tsetse flies, and the Morse lamps of fireflies
That bring the night sky to our grasp, no, only crickets chorus yes.

And that is enough for this ital dread even if his truth lies
Flat as a stone skipped on water for a glimpse of a prophet
Walking there with nothing but vapor for clothes and head hair.

4

My 5-year old asks the King what he keeps under his bonnet.
Is it an ostrich egg or is it a cotton wool ball? He smiles at her,
Utters a long, no, to both and says what's under there is a mole.

He names my 14-year old, Coconut Man, because he jiggled
Three coconuts from a tree held them at knifepoint and bored holes
For three glasses of sweet, milk water. Stuck in the middle,

My 11-year old, wants King David to name him too, so bets
On his Jamaican accent and a typical phrase from our intrepid
Guide: when rainfall all man high and low must get wet.

We are near our time to leave the island and King David.
We want to take him with us to keep him near us, even if
We know we cannot and must not interfere with a destiny

Each of us must make, and everyone must find alone in life,
With help as needed but not help forced out of pity.
Whatever King David wants from us sorrow would be last

On his list, just as the meal he conjured for us he offered
With his hands and from his heart to break our fast
From glut and deepen our understanding of the sufferers.

He shows us his receipt to run water from the main,
A down payment on one-third of the pipe that he needs.
From his license with his mug shot I see his former name,

Martin. From slavery, he says. Before her mother married,
My wife chips in, that her maiden name was Martin. What if
We're related? King David, guffaws, throws back his head,

And slaps the table, we are all one family, he says, chuffed
By the notion. He got his honorific from a toddler who saw
Him and christened him, King, and it stuck to his crown.

There is majesty in a housefly and in the dung at our feet
But we choose not to see it. In another life, his royal grounding,
Like Rodney, leads a country of loyal subjects in a lasting peace.

5

Each leaf, flower, bark and vine cures an ailment. All roots fetch
Remedies from soil to smooth our journey in this robber's era.
From I open my eyes I see glory days more than our mischief

And I give thanks for my part in all life in and out my area.
I am worth more than I think, in a life worth less than a germ.
I am lucky not to be absent from my mind like a baldhead.

All life flicks with a purpose and I mean to serve my term
As befits flesh that must toil for the kingdom of the righteous dead.
I cover my locks because I am an uprooted tree, roots up high,

Feeding on air as much as feeding air, and I walk as the stream
Of trees dictates, pollen brings back news of places that ships fly
Over the horizon to find, and I close my eyes at night with this dream:

Jah guides me through rough tides, and I swing thing and walk tall.
I bow down for no man. I want nothing besides this lean-to on a hill,
This taste of island air. I may look as if I perch and I man about to fall

But I stand strong with the poor - the world's most crowded windowsill.
I hold firm to the truth that since creation brethren read the scripture
Of the sea, pages turned by tides, waves stacked in a library

Whose spines are middle passage bones. The wind plaits ligatures
From the waves because the sea wants to be Rasta and Irie.
The forest smokes after a downpour, leaves rolled in a giant Rizla.

Evidence for what I am grows everywhere and I will always be heard.
I man godly, and the God of man is the Most High, Jah Rasta.
Upstairs, the deep turns charcoal. Insects shut down market. Birds

Tuck in wings for the night. Nails spill from a bucket, but it
Upturns and those nails hammer the galvanize, for a whole minute
Flat no room for any other thought. We just sit in that silence, and wait

In its haze, for the nails to drift off and leave behind these minute
Holes in pitched tarpaulin, whose faraway poles spin the brain's compass,
So that what's up, spirals down, that tree with dreads, unfazed and

Ready for anything, is King David, roots covered, his feet trespass
Nowhere, free to ride sea breeze and mountain air, free in his DNA.
We hug and promise to keep in touch and I say I will tell everyone

Who comes to the island to look for him for the time of their lives.
Blessings, he says, and we part. It tugs at me to leave him, so very alone
In his mercy, his bounty, and me, underdeveloped, ostensibly civilized.

CALL & RESPONSE

I

Dear Martin, I wish you had never been found.
Telescope and direction, aim, hammer, grudge,
Velocity and malice sent me, your bloodhound.
As I burned through space, left my own sound
In my wake, parted strands from my site, dodged
Time, split particles, my Hummingbird instant
For your slow, finger wet in mouth test of falling,
Swept aside by my speed inside your constant,
I knew where I would end up, what my blunt
Instrument must do to your routine, more calling
Than career, to that bigger dream you coined,
Robbed of you, grabbed by me, us joined.

I knew others would follow you in my name,
For no other reason than that my trade is grief,
I bear harm, win nothing, end warmth, halt fame.
I flew to you knowing violence would be blamed,
Not me, I saw all the things you did, your beliefs,
And so much more that you planned to do and say.
All the congregations and demonstrations headed
By you, all eyes on you, for your next word, prayer,
Song and lift of everybody up and into a new day,
Some place where words take you, where dread
Cannot enter, nor what I bring to put an end
To all your good, always it is me they send.

If self could be a case filled with powder, stifled
In steel, fired in a barrel, one word in my brain,
Kill, that was me who stared into the sight on his rifle,
Latched onto you, thought no more about your life
That Memphis morning in January at the Lorraine,
Your followers in the courtyard, you on a balcony.
I am hate. I have it stenciled in my manufacture.
 I dream of being the last thing to sow acrimony,
Stop love, yet here I am again in another testimony,
Of souls gathered worldwide to mark your departure,
No gladness, no air without duress, but your funeral
March to add to a life of marches, sermons, gone viral.

Forgive me, Martin. They sent me to start another war.
I do not age. I can only add to my hurts. I fight to keep
Grief as my condition, as if a Hummingbird tasted raw
Air brimming nectar, rather than the neck of flowers.
I remain the children in your big Washington speech,
Your dream stickles midstride, wings all wave and dart,
Black and white occupy space not on any timetable.
Sun and moon for tides in my pulse, if I had a heart
Like yours, so large for your chest crowds carry parts
For you, from your end through their time into fable
Without end, without me, or any relative in its face,
Not as a child or flesh and blood thing but as peace.

2

Rest in me. End your journey. Let my flesh be your bed
If you promise to sleep, never rise to erase another day.
Much like the one where you searched out my voice
On your blind drive to a different place, person, time.
Did you even notice the Memphis morning sky? Red.
Breakfast talk close with friends about our next play,
Workweek, public, cherishing last night when I stood
Before a congregation, said I knew great risk follows
This path of ours that I picked without luxury of choice
In my luck, my life, if fortune helps understand mine.
Speaking for myself, I said I did not want an easy road,
Even if gardens for those routes hummed with flowers,
Fruit, longevity, and every magnetic host up above,
Meaning here on earth, all that I know, want, love.

For here I am in front of you in a white shirt, my staple.
Chest may as well be bare in my stance to receive you.
Here comes my death as I taste the morning, exhale
My worst dreams from last night: that my life thief
Shimmies up to me and catches me; that all the people
Who hear how I leave them cannot believe it to be true,
Their Martin gone, stolen from them, and such crisis
Bring some good, somehow, hard to see as heads spin,
Hands, thrown out for balance, break linked arms, fail
Legs and we fall. I say, stop, even if you burst with grief.
My abrupt end triggers some greater good. Yes, I miss
My wife, children, congregation, this world I love like sin,
Love more than myself, though love of life counts for loss
Of self, as each of us tries for one or both, win or lose.

I fall in shock but without surprise that you appear
In an instant in the middle of everything. I want it now
No other way, no second chance, nor luck. Who prays
For my last stand? I leave my warm feet, remove
Myself, float, disperse, fall back, sprinkled, into ears,
Eyes, lips, nostrils, molecular, so that all who say I won,
Or ever heard my name, everyone born in my slip stream,
Cannot help but bear me, my body reversed, returned
To molecules, digitalized, cut loose as big data. I raise
My voice. I peel my eyes wide. I take in what takes over
Me when I talk, overcome, knowing if my faith means
I pay with my last breath. I pay. All of you, stay tuned,
Your nod, hail for me, more ready for me than my words
Were for me, for this time, where even a Hummingbird

Darts too slow to slip from your sight, your sound
Laced air, left far back, target in the act of falling,
Caparisoned, always this fall, as I, me, you, us, we, drop,
Never to land, save as code made by flesh and blood,
Art, yes, but not what flesh and blood were made for,
Lacerate my body with hardly a knock, more a drive
Through me to some other place, but at a cost to me
Getting where I stand in Memphis, where Tennessee
Happens to be on the globe, and my body, soaked in
Fever before I can think, hot, much less make sound,
Do much more than breathe out, as you divide my air
Between one Hummingbird wing beat and the next,
Rake into my body, drill deep, and whip my soul away,
Make my words and me, at thirty-nine, last and last.

BURNING PARADISE
for André Naffis-Sahely

1

They count our dead,
        Got no fucking warning.
They count one twice.
        Had to run out with no teeth, no nothing.
Count once, we said,
        But measure twice.

2

One road in, two ways out,
one for four wheels,
the other for off-roaders.

Big orange horizon drawing
near, embers sent ahead,
rosy barbecue smoke.

Some of us stumble
with our arms out,
falling into a hot embrace

that tightens the more
you wrestle to break free

3

I left my stack of books in a back bedroom whose door to
the backyard abuts Hummingbird feeder number one, where
many a wee flicker as Burns might put it, swoop at my head
so that I duck, squint and squeal.

We stand in the backyard with glasses filled with fermented
something or other and a gust drops in, makes us stop and
look up as it assumes the dimensions of three majestic pines
only to crack a whip at the oak whose limb breaks onto that
makeshift gazebo where many grilled meals graced us in its
closeted confines, just upgraded with new frame, fresh tarp
and bright year-round holiday lights.

Your cat's grave in the right corner near the back fence with
a stone marker and daffodils, as if each step taken by that
ancient lovely, fur ball, as we called him (that you took in as a
stray, more person than cat, who crawled up to you wrapped
in his thick blanket and the purr of a Lamborghini) each paw
print, pressed and buried a bulb that sprouted this trail of
yellow.

Sunsets we walk out your gate, turn right and head to the
end of the road and back taking note of each lot, every minor
pothole in the road and the way the light hides behind trees
and runs as we approach.

I push past easy recall, back to a time when deer broke
through the bamboo fence trim around your vegetable
garden, and pilfered lettuce, Persian cucumber, cherry tomato.
I look early one morning at how our wire repairs of replaced
bamboo stay in place and no more deer try to break in for
reasons I put down to your spell issued as a silent prayer.

4

Halfway down Skyway a sign says scenic view and warns
motorists about 1000 yards away to consider stopping. If you
pull off the two downward lanes there is this mini canyon
that draws your eyes out of your head.

The giddy descent opens what seems like half a mile
of rugged land with an equal drama of rising rock and
vegetation on the far side. The valley swoops away in
competition with the excavated sky.

Deep below in between rocks and hidden by trees, a river –
of course, what else – twists over stones. The thinnest breeze
lifts the river sky high.

Bedroom window
window gravel driveway
driveway pine-shaped sky
sky that sun peeps
peeps through at dawn
dawn that stripes gold
gold at dusk

pines decorated
with crows
so many black
fruit settled
out of reach
cackle raucously

5

Singed dog
                    trots up to us
                                        wagging
strange dog so
                    friendly
                                        he seemed to know us
from a life
                    we gave up
                                        in a hurry
involuntarily

6

Not the red skin of a sky
nor the wind flexing muscles

        this sky skinned red
        wind too strong to breathe

not the drop of night to cancel our day
nor the birds that fall on our shoulders

        this dark so thick
        we can't cut through

flocks calling heavenly bodies
that we cannot see calling

7

Trees talk

We shape the wind
we make the light

wind that shapes us
light that makes us

we fan the flames
we feed the flames

flames that meet us
greet and eat us

make us ash
take to air

trees of embers
pollen embers

trees of cloud
roots everywhere

8

Ash poured for a foundation
where a building stood
tree turned coal
as if a seam underground
ten floors high
mined to exhaustion
left these surface sentinels

9

Birdless scorched earth
if what tore through here
could be named as anything

devil hit us so hard so fast
stone exploded left our brick
firesides standing with nothing
else around meaning the whole

house reduced to bricklayers
ash whose color drained us
dry so that we became ashen
guided by our automatic feet

we count our dead they count
one twice cut once we said
but measure twice

10

The controversial orange leader
helicoptered into our leveled
town to show
solidarity
with us
who lost every thing

His tongue lashed
our poor upkeep of our forest

He held up Finnish
habit of combing
forest free of brush

They shook heads
at his use of them
to lambast us
up to our ankles in ash

Who called our town
by the wrong name
Pleasure not once
but twice
and left us
empty handed
minds scraped
like calabash

All we have left
is a curse
for a spell

Come back fire
do for orange
what you did for us

Do that and we
forgive your trespass
as our original trespass
into indigenous forest
these indigenous hills
this indigenous valley

11

From this day
  eat all food
 cold from tin
   shrink-wrap or foil

All the child has to do is run to you as you call her and wave
your arms, curl them, from outstretched, back to your chest,
and out again, calling her, come child, you're safe now, come
to me, be quick, come, here, your arms held out to her and
waving her to your embrace.

  From this day
   live in winter
   do not crave
  marshmallows by open – (delete)

But she watches your lips move and does not seem to read
them or hear a word. She stares at your arms' semaphore with
a blank look of not knowing what it means to wave her to
you for her own good. She looks over her shoulder at what
chases her to this point and what seems about to sweep her
up into its embrace.

  Do not strike
   a match
     for its brilliant – (delete)
   delete all
  associations with –

Rather than turn from it and run to you as you call to her
and as your arms beckon her to do the child twists around in
the direction of her backward glance and as you shout no, do

not, please, child, come this way to me, before you get half of
that out of your mouth, your arms wide for her, she vanishes.

> Into the arms of that thing
>   without a name
>   from the earth to the sky
>   from this day
>   that thing
>   that shall remain
> nameless

12

The child, with nowhere to run, no place to hide, is all of us.
Outpaced, we abandon our cars and the cats and dogs inside
the closed car windows as the boiling air runs up to us. That
child peels from my skin and falls behind and I find myself
turning around to face that child now some way behind me.
I beg her to come back to me never mind the fact that I am
the one who flees from her.

13

we drove to the top of the hill
inhabited the name of our town
parked in cloud planted among trees

when we were up brethren
sistren we were high
there was no halfway up

just this no person land
this crow's lookout
neither up nor down

14

the beauty of the nightmare in the way
what looks like fireflies swarmed the trees
occupied every opening
ring-o roses
smuts of red light ferried by the wind
locust storm of lightning bugs
touch down with a burning kiss
ring-o roses

so that everything went up
ring-o roses everything turned ash

15

No deluge to grace
our powdered bones
no clip-clop-pitter-patter

canticle of water
to soothe what's left of this town
crows scare and strip pines of fruit

unsettled, our spirits run
leave scorched ground
always homeward bound

LETTERS TO AMERICA (AN ABECEDARY)
for Yogita and Anish

'Ah neva seen this before in all ma years.'
Testify, Sis. How we grew accustomed,
Spoiled almost, by decorum, now try
Mosquito larvae cultivating at speed
In standing bodies of water. pigeons
Flock rooftops, twist, launch, shout
As one, spin sky, turn skulls porous.

Car repair shop drills sing industry.
Tires feel out parking, meters freed.
First horn blare triggers this chorus.
Step up pistons, fire motor mouths,
Say our only worry is our worst fears
Come true. Mosquito straw proboscis
Drinks from my arm, bam! Adios asterisk.

*

But, really, am I eyeballing an armored truck?
Says one dung beetle to half earthworm,
Who replies, as Gloucester, I see it feelingly.

Who gave those uniforms permission to storm
School car parks, automatics drawn? Finches ask
Robins, who, channeling Auden, whistle —

Bang! WTF!

Bang, bang, Lulu, Lulu gone …

The calypso worked its juju
On my digital radio.

Flags at half-mast for this Union.
Taps on trumpets dawn till dusk.
Guides, Scouts, look out for rainbows

Projected on a disused warehouse in LA County.
Clocks throughout the land tell one contiguous time.
Rain and shine stop dead in tracks on borderlines.

*

Cat asks me if dogs can ever be cool.
After two of my kind pin down one of his
On a front porch until chased off by our rulers.

I open my mouth to spit some piety about
Lions lying down with lambs but only bark
What my genes say I should, ears pulled back.

Do you remember Judas Iscariot? Thirty silver
Pieces and a certain last supper just for this.
A taser for every problem warns the bee

With an empty bonnet, sting for emphasis,
About why one plus one never makes two,
After voting from sea to oil-slicked sea.

Look at her, look at him, hold, kiss babies
In photo ops, all gaga, minus bathtub
Never mind water, in this national soap,

This wait for the next sentence whose weight
'Illegals' carry on shoulders they look over
Nonstop, even in sleep, one eye open,

Breath held when police cruise by,
Car backfire skin jump heartbeat skip,
Day in, day out, glory hallelujah, do I have

A witness as empire zips into bonfire.
For what? To dip wrists in fresh water
From an inverted fountain in a square.

*

Black lives matter but blue lives matter more. Duh.
Veins, blue, blood, plus or minus, B this or A that.
Epicurus, I find your coin staring up at me
From the bottom of my beer mug, too late
For Troy, for Trayvon. I need a flotation device, A buoy, Woolf's
lighthouse and single room Garvey's Star Line to beam me up Scotty.

Where is yesteryear's full moon that silvered Towers and made a
midnight lake of the city Where lovers strolled, hand in hand, one
black, One white, with no mind for anyone and no two Minds in
their business? Gone the way of drones Whose shadows crossed the
moon without trace On GPS to sow grief in the name of cod, liver, oil.

Spell it out or risk talk stuck in ecofriendly caves.
Black and blue, both, why can't we, intoned,
Rodney (not Walter), get along? Because,
Because, because (fill in the dots) with your
Trotsky (or Brodsky) and your Marx (Groucho).
Laugh therapy narrows eyes, blocks ears,
Hurts jaws, ribs, merrily, merrily, cha-cha. Cha.

Eek-A-Mouse blasts my buds, as I read
The instruction manual, which says
One thing but leads to another
When I piece it together, finally.
It being the thing I refuse to name.

My nerves, porous as that strainer
I hold over a tilted pot full of spaghetti
In hot water. Pavarotti, in the shower
Malcolm before a cracked mirror,
Gaga at each news item competing

For part Fool. Ornate, abandoned nest
Left in place, in my suburban rafter,
Squirreled from without a note,
Unless feathers could ever be a sign
Of things to come, of what once was.

*

Face Beckett's door, imperceptibly ajar.

His stage direction, for how things
Turn out here if this show goes on.

Sir Ian, why reserve your last check
For your flies, before you take the stage?
Because all eyes alight there first.
Mr Spock, where is the logic in this?

I marvel at comics from my youth
In 4K, LED. Captain, put me ashore.

By which I mean at sea with sirens,
Ears unwaxed, sternum lashed to bow.

What is your name? Kunta. Whip.
Am I not a ... asked Sizwe in Fugard.
You are trans, on loan from genes,
Dust, waves, particles, here, today.

*

Go-go in la-la land whines craft for art's saké.
See that chrysalis hanging like a mural.
Should it stop unfolding, hold back
Dues, suspend when wings peel gloves,
Snake free, take flight, remind the greed
In our chi, Che, cha, what turns without
Turning? If you must know, but first,

Shush, write milk in lemon juice on foolscap,
Read by passing over Bunsen. Mercurial
Chemists, we were all Curie. Cooked crack
Ready to pay any price, to find out if love
Could ever be a portion, all you would need,
To spin Mercator a tad faster on whiteout
Poles, match our heart, tap, rat-a-tat burst.

*

1. Hummingbird feeder needs refill
2. Peel sticker, off window, that says glass
3. Buy T-shirt with directive, mind the gap

4. Sip tea from mug, of civil rights dead
5. Breathe in, sure, but really exhale
6. Note how breeze lifts a whole branch
7. Whose green skirt shows white undies

*

I mean certain legends about flight that grow up with right minds to help them come to terms with change that may be out of their control. Lone branch ranges from a curved palm 90 feet over LA's 1914 craftsman in historic Adams.

How flayed branch cruises broadcasts a specific gravity geared to flight of the right kind, slow, bracing, reluctant, noncommittal, inevitable, and resigned to its fate.

Through double-glazing I hear, so I believe, that swoosh of storied capital decline, swish perhaps, almost a whistle, as you wish, much like us as kids with a clasped blade of grass held to our pursed lips for that didgeridoo that was elevator music to us atonal types.

But how can a branch sing if made to move on by wind and rain from where it began, and thought it would end, even if a philosophy spread among shoots of a final sail set for another dimension?

As word of government raids spread through town and university we forwarded emails, Instagrams, and stopped with neighbors in streets to exchange the latest.

Is this time for emergency measures or are we too blind to

know what we can feel coming a mile away, where someone
who knows someone we know stops for bread, milk, eggs
and is grabbed, handcuffed, and carted off to detention?

Imagine us as branches dislodged in a sea change helped by
soft water. We cling, not to give up on all we know. What
for? That fall, we must accept as fate.

*

Juggernaut ancestors shape-shift cumulus,
March across dull blue grass to bagpipes.

Change bandages on Grandmother.
Amputated right hand she says she feels

Rainy days in Georgetown as a firm handshake
That rattles all 27 phantom bones, makes her shiver.

Grandfather never averts his bifurcated lens
From his Golden Treasury, unless his hanky readies

To catch eyewater at the blurred sight of her.
In a time of airships, of toothpicks operated

Behind hand cover. Whoever you vote for,
(Runs the calypso) the government gets in,

Ting-a-ling-a-ling. Doan tek serious thing
Mek joke, bannoh. WTF. Twin towers got us

Here. Nah, Reagan. Nope, slavery. Try again.
Irony, that republic of deferred action.

Hummingbird smashes into that glass door,
My mother walks absently into it too.

I glance just in time, brake and catch a face
That I look through to my final destination.

*

K Street in South London?
Now? How? One morning at 6:30
I crossed Blackheath Hill.

On my paper round
Met a scrawny fox halfway
Uphill, down, not sure

We paused, inhaled each
Other, fox-trotted away,
In a slight panic,

Me thinking tabloid
Headlines, rabid animal
Chases paper kid

On delivery route.
Follow as I buzz myself
Into a tower,

Board elevator, a man
In a suit exits,
With the merest nod.

Climb 8 floors, carry
That fox, and just as I plunge
The folded Mirror

Into letter box,
Door, ajar, flies open, wham!

A very pregnant
Woman, naked, swollen breasts
Blazing redhead, small

Burning bush at crotch,
Fills doorframe, scrambles my head.
She takes one moment

To compute I am
Not her partner, slams door, smack,
In my wide-eyed face.

That moment, as she
Processes me and I her,
Stretches out enough

For me to see her
Shoulder-length, red, flaming curls
And inverted red

Triangle tuft at her crotch,
Bright stretched skin at her
Distended navel,

An outie, as though
I crashed at high speed and could
Recall the lead up

Frame by stark frame for
Posterity, mine and hers,
Her child near its term.

The rest of my round
I peer left, right, near distance,
Round bends, for said fox.

I conjure woman,
Pregnant, framed by her threshold,
Here, now, with only

Me, you, these measures,
This emergency, all three,
To foster, connect all.

                *

Lap up 70s Airy Hall, Guyana.
One road in and one road out,
One of everything village,
Caiman, donkey, peacock,
And mad expat Englishman
Footloose and fancy-free
Who we stone with red sand
That crumbles on contact
Grabbed from the roadside
That acts as giant bow,
Strung with two-story house,
Whose Greenheart frame,
Tensed, held all this time.
English pelted for saying,
Down his big burnt nose,
That he was sent here

To rule us half-clad children
That he in his better days
Seeing better times before
Guyana's famous red rum
Got the better of him,
Helped sow high and low,
And everything between
Our town and country.

                        *

Maestro, we played, shoots
Planted in one place
Sprouts in disorderly rows,
Up whole feet if you look away
For a spell, all loaded
In one hammock strung

Between rafters in a back room
Empty until harvest
Stuffed paddy from roof

To pillar to post.
Rice husk smell for days.
Rocking chair song and dance

On full moons, donkey-bray
At midday, peacock-scream
Various most afternoons.

                        *

Now help bring barefoot
pale instep, cracked heel,

stamping Englishman
back, not to curse,
stone or ridicule, but to hear
how he would remedy this now
so out of sync with then.

*

Once more help us

*

Parse wheat from chaff,

*

Quantify this voting

*

Result that tests our gall

*

Stepped-on alligator, Uncle

*

Takes for a log bridge

*

Until it lifts, shakes, yawns.

*

Velocity of legs cycling air,
Caiman, not alligator,
Lassoed between two poles,
Fetched back to the house,
Cut loose in a fenced field
For sport for that day,
Lost to me every day since.
I bring it back, steady
Its shine, against this time,

*

Where I am told one past
Counts most, all others
Must be put down to what
That alligator, jaws agape,
Head reared, ur-present,
Ready to lash with tail,
Charge at anyone
Who takes it for a log.

*

X marks the spot where
Englishman walks in half
Circles, pumps his bent
Arms as if to fly, cackles
Like a peacock, only to get
The real thing started,
The two in a quarrel thrice
Removed from that magic
Flower duet from Lakmé

By Léo Delibes. Peacock,
Donkey, caiman, village fool,
Be my ally, bring it all,
Cow, moon, dish, spoon.

*

Yo-Yo Ma follows Eek
On democracy's Shuffle Play.

*

Zebra asks me in Queen's
English peppered with Esperanto

If he be black whiff white stripes
Or white wid black stripes.

I wake with this atonal pair
On the edge of my edginess:

'I do not care, I do not care,
If the Don has on underwear.'

'But don't you think or worry some,
That his nudity is zero sum?'

'I cannot see for the life of me,
Why that should concern anybody.'

'I fret when all's said and done,
We leave him be, he has his fun.'

CALYPSO

I

Calypso king bounce back after an absent spell,
I know you miss his wisdom and his testy smell.
He got an aroma that lingers like an empire.
All you crave his bohemian lyrics, their rapid fire.
I only come in answer to your desperate call
For a jester with cahones to address this squall
Between a global monster and a flea outpost
Resisting the overtures of empire brute force,
Between Brexiteers frogmarched by idealogues
Versus Europhiles always open for dialogue,
The resurgence globally of the far right
Shooting up schools and holy sites.
Marx must be turning in his Highgate grave
For the class that surplus value could not save.
For each gripe I got rhymes coming out my pores,
More than Microsoft Windows have doors,
Or Amazon with its forest of packages,
Or Facebook with its eyes on all ages,
More than government bank bailouts
While CEOs refuse to take pay cuts,
And election corporate tax breaks
Line deep pockets as the breadless eat steak.
Politicians decide in the people's domain,
God and big business to kick some foreign
Backside, but what they trust and worship
More than any just cause or shiny battleship,
Happens to be paper and green, with the onus
Less on The Almighty than on a hefty bonus.
Their forced aid amounts to a flimsy plaster
Slapped on cuts that just bleed faster

Everyday; we being the Third World, so
-called, the ones shipped west to reap and sow
As slaves. What history left us there's no cure
For, or if there is one, as Diana's song implores,
We don't want it, stick it, index it with plunder,
Western leaders keep our beelike cause under
Your queen beds until we ripe to come
Out and sting every developed, moving thing some
Board reckoned on turning into a handsome profit.
For all the pain your democracy dish out – stop it!
We can't stomach your sugarcoated pills anymore,
You murder us with interest and we still poor.
In my last life I blazed a trail of vinyl tracks
(Turntables had needles that really scratched
Before scratching records became Ice Cube cool
And they classed my inventions as old dude school.)
Laying down how the very rich turned playing fair
Into a circus: give them a yard they grab a hectare.
The Empire break up, so I breaking it down,
Exposing all them politicians acting the clown,
But behind we back they brandishing knife
Swearing they love Black as they take our life,
Or should that be wife, son or daughter,
Politics and religion equal poor folk slaughter.
The spirituality every humble person needs
Got sweet FA to do with a make money creed.
The poor extract the spiritual from the simplest acts
Such as helping a neighbor or any scratch-my-back
And-I'll-scratch-yours gesture; a little thing that deep
Shows the poor own power. Why should they be meek?
Many ants make an army, one weak, many strong.
The day ants grasp their strength that day anteaters gone.
Pardon my doomsday-calypso-singer persona.
I sold platinum when the message was the medium, Sonny.

I try to keep my humor nevertheless, I try to laugh
Like everybody else, I lime, labrish, hang and gaff.
But there comes a time when a body must speak
Headlines, when body should not turn the other cheek:
THIS PROLONGED WAR FOR OIL AND REVENGE
FOR NINE-ELEVEN FOUNDED ON TOO MANY LIES
AND COST TOO MANY LIVING.
Empire building for profit margin should be exposed –
Paine gone bad when used for company expos.
Corporate types with mansions and stretched limos,
Stretch Paine's logic on the rack; these doyens
Of global trade covert Paine to pounds, dollars and yen.
A rubber necklace's too kind and colloquial an end for
Buzzards that feed on honest, local vendors.

2

The Caribbean's pearls scattered from a necklace
Some sea goddess broke when she tossed her face
Towards the sun to clear seaweed that strayed
Over her eyes, she cursed the place and the curse stayed
Since it was a goddess who said it, and Europeans
Discovered the beads and cleansed them of Amerindians.
And because theirs was a different kind of curse
Europeans brought back the blight with centuries
Of enslaved Africans, indentured Asians.
When I stare into the Caribbean basin
I see that same goddess brewing a storm of grief
For her curse that lasted so long from an act so brief
As an off-the-cuff utterance. Now there's a god
For the bad weather that rips trees off the tripods
Of postcards worked by the offspring of slaves,
From civilization's cradle to civilization's grave.

Don't pity the poor in your lavish art of piety,
They will watch you bleed after cutting your artery.
Give them something they can use to better their lot:
Bob Marley's small axe, his big hat over copious locks.
He gelled epistle and liturgy as a rasta-reggae prophet,
When he Chant Down Babylon, power lines atrophy.
His songs cover poor people, he's their champion,
History was his caviar, poverty his champagne,
Ideas pop in his head, lyrics flow from his mouth;
Marley's the seer thirsty minds should know about.

You hear the government news? A man ask
Me the other day. I take my time to dress down the ass,
How can you mix government and new in one breath?
He spit back, You open yuh mouth and ah smell death.
Even I feel bad sometimes, I want to crumble,
But some thing in me always ready to rumble.
When I catch idle talk about politics like it new,
I come to the boil and start to fret and stew
About how politics with its polymorphous tricks
Pretend to walk soft but mostly wield a cocomacca stick.
Ain't change since Rome when Caesar fall to Brutus
And Nero fiddled at home; all that trickle down to us
Like it happen yesterday. Sun and moon share space
But new and government make me shout disgrace.

3

On the Peter's Projection America's a smear
On the blue ocean planet's steamy underwear.
American power and American might in a century
Of nuclear fright, amounts to a skid mark on greenery
Left out of the fridge to wilt. I mean to say as plain

As my tongue can spell it that America dish out pain
While the rest of the world must swallow for the sake
Of world peace, as parents, trying to accommodate
A spoiled brat having a giant, orange-faced tantrum,
Throw up hands and watch since what's to be done?
Parental hands wringing on the sidelines did not settle
Well with students whose Internet savvy upset Seattle.
They threw projectiles at the G-summit accord,
Made the evening news and got a police record.
It takes the youth to remind us of basic decency.
They crossed the bigwigs who showed no leniency
When it came to stamping out democratic protest,
Quick to deploy Marcuse's state repressive apparatus.
What's gross about America remains its excesses:
What bulge, super-size egos and thirst for gasses.
They should bottle the stuff their leader tweets all night
While on the can, if only hybrids can run on tripe.
The rest of us mortals can't take anymore, please,
Stuffed to the gills from America's emission and sneeze.

This in no way exonerates the small-island nation,
Those elites in the over-governed Caribbean basin
Who fly wide-eyed into the trap of consumption
With shopping sprees to New York, Miami, London,
While their country's majority lack two red cents
To cover dead eyes, rulers mortgage the innocents
Tied to high-interest loans from the IMF and World Bank,
Stuck in vaulted back pockets for life, which, thank
Goodness, is not forever. So pour the rum and let
The music play, we got life now, forgive and forget.

I can't help thinking about Africa's plight,
Aids, war, post-colonial rule, and no daylight
Between western elites and their home grown progeny,

Both jet to Harrods and breakfast at Tiffany's.
Africa pulls on my heartstrings more than I can name,
More than any place, Africa's the diaspora's shame,
Our hurt when we got nothing to complain about
But can't fathom why sleep won't start after lights out.
Children beckon with limbs lopped off by freedom fighters,
Blood sparkles in the conscience of diamond gatherers,
Tribes war over borders drawn up in 1885 in a plot
That slashed the face of Africa with the artificial blot
Of borders, like history's fool Africa gets played
Like a celibate priest who just wanna get laid.
Africa, cradle of our species, oh Africa, skull in profile,
Mercator mapped. Africa, the child; Europe, the pedophile.

4

Don't make me rant, stop me before the calypso spoil,
Don't stand there pop-eyed, while I pitch Cod Liver Oil.
Lend a hand; join the band; beat some pan; show me hope.
My tongue is my instrument. Let me bubble like soap.
My bones ground to dust; watch me, I'm almost a fossil.
Two stones mark the spot where populations bustled
In my thighs, two more for my jellyroll eyes
Which woke, saw, recorded, closed then vaporized.
I aim to come back stronger than curry that goes in hot
But comes out hotter. Don't rush me. This is my slot.
Rush me if you Russian. Hurry, hurry, mek bad curry.
As a watched pot never boils so a calypso won't flurry
If Lot's wife's worth her salt or gestalt as the case may be;
Keep up if you can, I switch from politics to psychology.
Ear to the ground, tongue in my cheek, glint in my eye;
Sway in my hips, my fingers click; you laugh till you cry.
I'm in the driving seat so my eyes need to be clear,
Otherwise trouble, nobody going anywhere

Fast, we one plait on one head of a scalp of thick hair
See that and avoid ideological catacombs of living dead,
Learn from Afros, locks and canerows of political heads,
Even bald heads in top hats dream hair long as twine.
Lyrics keep flowing with the beer, spirits and times.

I take the back route since I done dead already,
I pick up roots and shake my head like Solomon Grundy.
I play the part Sir John Harrington played for hygiene,
Except my throne rules the moral and ethical scene.
He invented the toilet, I invoke satire; between us two
We prop your hind quarters higher, ask Swift or Miss Lou.
I coming to face the moral Lilliputians like a Gulliver,
Like the ads say about the rock and roll pizza, I deliver.
I lift people's collective spirit and cleanse their soul,
I wake eyes, soften ears, so mind, prepare to get scold,
A scalding of the character, a whipping back into shape,
A butt-kick of the highest order, not a soul escapes.

Daylight on the city, once I visit, looks spic and span,
The national grid, polished by ethics, arranged for pan.
I empty churches (confessionals with nothing doing,
Just whispers) I provide people moral gluing.
Nuff said 'bout me, one more thing on the climate,
My mission's to lift us above our cousins the primates,
Won't end with my song, not for long if we're to win
Against corporate malfeasance and out and out sin
Committed by governments who dispose of our young
In armies of conquest for greased palms, oil towns.
By the time I stop this, how many babies will die
From diseases we can cure? So many children lie
On dirt floors and stop brushing gangs of flies
From their cracked mouths and empty eyes.
Too many for my liking, too many to excuse,

Each of us makes a choice to ignore or choose
To do some small thing, over and above despair,
We can vote, write, place calls, march and cheer.
If the revolution must stream by phone and TV
Let it be on time, on our terms and commercial free.
Let the red wounds of roses in vases of gun barrels
Look like a real possibility that could end quarrels
Rather than optioned for a film, t-shirt and chain
Store like Che, the holocaust, Palestinians, the rain
Forest. I could go on, I will just a little longer:
Rhetoric is a poison that makes reason stronger.
But only because the times make me turn all grave;
The children, the innocents, need to be saved
From the consumption monster capitalism,
Consumer of the planet till the planet capitulates.
Join hands and sing with me, we shall overcome,
The will of the people adds up to a powerful sum.
Draw a line in the sand; let's make that last stand,
For the benefit of all species sharing common land.

5

I know when I strike this note you hear pure Lennon.
I realize many poets consider politics a bit of a lemon.
But I past caring about what others think, those who try
To write but don't read, poets who plant their poetry
In commerce, who lack hearts and don't give a farthing
About anyone; who vacate morality from all things art,
For some privileged notion of self exploration and some
Heady hunch that their art's private: it's only (as one
Private said to another about army life) as private as our
Privates; poets navel-gazing abdication of the Muse, sours
The tried and true calling to bear witness to what
We sense, must say, no matter how little lands in our hats.

Poetry requires us to cuddle wasps, speak in tongues
On behalf of the downtrodden, to the hard ears of big guns.
I say this with a crystal memory of falling in love
With a woman who I could not get enough of
Nor she of me; our world revolved around the bedroom,
We filled each other's head, swept cobwebs with a broom
Of desire that lit our bodies with a perpetual fire and thirst
For each other, so much so I felt I was going to burst
With happiness, I felt blessed and worried the flame
Would die and I'd never find this kind of love again.
And it did run out but not because anything died inside
It was just that the everyday has a way you can't hide
From for long, of encroaching, as the mundane
Keeps up its reminders of the, well, yes, mundane.
Love isn't all you need but love turns us topsy-turvy,
Love butters the heart and stuffs its bread in the belly.
At any point during that affair I felt I could face an army
For a cause or for nothing, I mean contented, dreamy.
Love is a bug that infects flesh, mind and spirit.
Desire turns viral and wrecks the body's habits.
Once you've loved that deep it's hard to settle for less.
You keep looking for the holy grail of earthly happiness.
Then you start to see the world falling short on every count
And bam! Before you know where you are you've mounted
Some public statue in a square and it's about to fall
To herald in some new day in some free for all.
Call it politics or opportunism, call it what you must,
But it's built on love and love is all I can trust
In this life to bring about what I can't see for all the wealth
In this world, but what I feel has to happen for the health
Of the planet: the prudent use of nature's finite resource,
And the countless poor, helped till they become scarce.

6

I must confess love kept me from politics with its drug.
I turned mushy in the head and lifeless as a rug.
It wasn't until I had my fill of the woman and her island
Ways that I began to notice headlines from other lands.
One picture of a naked Iraqi on the end of a girl-soldier's
Leash and one word, Guantanamo, started solder
From my eyes, more news trickled into my porous head
And like a sponge I began to soak it up and feel bad,
For Dharfur, for all thirty-three shot where I teach,
For Haiti and Japan's quakes with fallout in the streets,
For the woman-soldier, for Abu Graheb's void space.
I wanted each volunteer to answer but above all I placed
Full weight on government shoulders that could
Find no better use for the youth than fodder, firewood.

She begged me to stay, held my thighs as I walked off
Shaking my legs free. I ignored tingles, the warmth of
My loaded groin, watering tongue and giddy head.
She stopped calling my name and cursed me instead:
'May you never find pussy as sweet again but sour
Every time you go down for a taste, may you cry for
Its bliss but all you goin' get is a second rate squeeze
And nothing but missionary for your sins and diseased
Heart; may your seed always fall fallow and arms ache
From rolling your frustrated issue off your wrist
Into the dry bed of a tissue or into a shower's hiss,
May you ache for child but only get doubt and a mistake
To care for and nothing of your own but a stake
In your heart for me and what I offered, what you threw
Away.' That was the last I saw her. Every word came true.
I think of her when I hold another and I come up sour
Mouthed and impatient to finish and grab a few hours.

I tried for children for years until I fooled my mind
That the years were just days and I had bags of time
When the clock was about to run out with my options
And my drawstring seed sack dry up its populations.
I dived into party politics and bore all the cost
As compensation for love found and love lost
Through my fault and no one to blame not even
The government who had nothing to do with me leaving
Her when I did in answer to a call without origination
Or end, the call of my conscience whose tintinnabulation
Won't be ignored without a knot forming in the stomach,
One you can't untie or fool or decorate or flummox.

7

Most days the Atlantic unlocks vaults of silver coins,
Undersea light bends over backwards in benediction
To an element whose unmade bed of white bones,
Of Africans thrown overboard, form a road back home,
Back, back, back to Africa and some museum repose
In the wounded minds of the diaspora, those
Who cannot hear the too-high pitch of the notes
Of reconciliation without Queen Mother Moore's vote.
It's a current I tread in my sleep and the bones don't mind
My feet on them, in fact, they hold still for my kind
Who come in search of peace and find we can hold
Our breaths underwater and make our way to pots of gold
At the end of ancestral rainbows with politics, and love,
Birth of the Cool, rather than any nation or a God above,
As our guide, and the moral of the story is the story
Itself and there's no history without this morality.

I say me tuppence and I thank you for the loan
Of your ear and heart now leave me alone,

Set me free of bureaucracy and bad omens,
Let me meet my love, the only woman
Who made the wait of long months pass in a day
With the welcome weight of Tapper Zukie and L.K.J.
That she played and said nothing except to undo
Her curse and then my buttons, zip and you
Can imagine the rest, and if not, think of wreaths,
A reef knot of limbs, a Bombay mix of breaths.